For Tom

First published 1983 by
Walker Books Ltd,
17-19 Hanway House,
Hanway Place, London W1P 9DL

© 1983 Helen Oxenbury

First printed 1983
Printed and bound by
L.E.G.O., Vicenza, Italy

British Library Cataloguing in Publication Data
Oxenbury, Helen
Eating out. – (First picture books)
I. Title
823'.914 [F]   PZ7

ISBN 0-7445-0037-0

Eating Out

Helen Oxenbury

WALKER BOOKS
LONDON

Mum said, 'I'm too tired
to cook.'
Dad said, 'I'll take you
out for supper.'

'I suppose you need a high
chair,' the waiter said.
The room was hot and stuffy.

We had to wait ages
for the food.
'Why can't you sit still
like those nice little
children?' Dad said.

'Get back on your chair,'
Mum said. 'Here comes
your lovely meal.'

'Why didn't you say you
wanted to go before the
food arrived?' Mum said.

I wasn't very hungry,
so I went under the table.
Someone trod on my foot.

The waiter made a terrible mess.

'That's that,' Dad said.
'Never again,' said Mum.
'Anyway, I like eating at
home the best,' I said.